Table of Contents

Page

Preface

As of July 2004, there have been over 31,900 reserve Marines activated in support of the GWOT, the highest total since the Korean War. Yet with the current active duty operations tempo equating to a greater then one-to-one ratio, the Marine Reserve F/A-18 squadrons remain the only Reserve capability not to have been activated.

In light of the Department of Defense's push for transformation, and in the simple fact that not a single Marine Reserve F/A-18 squadron has been used in either Operation Enduring Freedom or Operation Iraqi Freedom, the following question must be asked: Are the Marine Reserve F/A-18 squadrons relevant? If they are relevant, then why, to date, have these Reserve squadrons not been used in the GWOT? If these squadrons are not relevant, then what should the Marine Corps do with them?

In providing the answers to the above questions, this research concludes that the Reserve F/A-18 squadrons are in fact relevant. Subsequently, five courses of action are offered as recommendations for the Marine Corps leadership, which if implemented, will significantly improve the use of these assets.

In fact, in January 2005, at about the time the first draft of this paper was to be completed, Headquarters Marine Corps made the decision to activate VMFA-142 for use in Operation Iraqi Freedom. Coincidently, in making better use of the Reserve F/A-18 squadrons, Marine Leadership implemented this papers recommended course-of-action. Sometime in March of 2005 this squadron will deploy as the first Marine Reserve TacAir squadron to support a contingency operation since the Korean War. Although I would like to believe the inquiries I made to Headquarters Marine Corps played a part in this decision, the reality is I doubt that they did. Even so, this paper provides a long-term look at the personnel problems posed by the Global War on Terror and offers some solutions to help mitigate their impact.

I would like to take the opportunity to thank those who were instrumental in enabling me to complete this research project. First and foremost is my wife and children; their patience and support were unwavering. I must also thank my two Marine Corps Command and Staff faculty advisors, Colonel "Nut-z" Niblock (USMC) and Dr. John Gordon, for their tutelage, guidance, and editing as I proceeded throughout this project. Finally, I would like to thank all the senior Marine Corps leaders who granted me interviews. They helped me to better understand the issues involved with my topic: LtGen Amos, MGen Bergman, MGen Ghormely, BGen Post, Col Brady, Col Blalock, Col Hawkins, Col Morey, LtCol Hitchcock, and Maj Roach, each of whom dedicated time from their busy schedules to answer my questions. I will be forever grateful.

MARINE RESERVE F/A-18 SQUADRONS; USE THEM OR LOSE THEM: THE ROLE OF 4th MAW F/A-18 SQUADRONS IN THE GOLBAL WAR ON TERROR

> *"Every dollar of defense spending must meet a single test: It must help us build the decisive power we will need to win the wars of the future."*
>
> *--George W. Bush*
> *Commander in Chief*
>
> *"With regard to the Reserves [in the context of the Global War on Terror], we have to do what's best for the institution, we can't afford to have forces sitting on the shelf."*
>
> *--LtGen James F. Amos, USMC*
> *Commanding General II MEF*
>
> *"We should take a very hard look at those units that were not used during Desert Shield/Desert Storm, that were not used in operations Enduring Freedom and Iraqi Freedom, or during the 90's as operational tempo relief, and ask ourselves the hard question: 'Are they necessary and what would be more relevant and useful if they aren't necessary?'"*
>
> *--MGen Arnold L. Punaro, USMCR (Ret)*
> *Former Director, Reserve Affairs*

INTRODUCTION

Currently, America and her coalition partners are at the three and a half year point in the extensive Global War on Terror (GWOT). Due to the extended nature of this irregular type of warfare, there is a tremendous amount of stress being placed on the American military's total force structure and the military is therefore finding itself in uncharted territory. As of July 2004, there have been over 31,900 Reserve Marines activated in support of the GWOT, eclipsing the Desert Storm total of 30,586.[1] The

---

[1] Adam Tustin, "Reserve Activations Reach Highest Since Korea," July 2004, *Marine Forces Reserve Home Page*, www.mfr.usmc.mil, web page URL http://www.marforres.usmc.mil/Archive/2004.07/activations.html, accessed 13 August 2004. Cited hereafter as Tustin.

numbers of activations have exceeded the high totals of the Korean War. "We've been activating, deactivating, and then reactivating to get as much life out of our units as possible," said LtCol Keith Hulet, director of manpower for Marine Forces Reserve.[2] Yet with over 70% of the Active duty Marine F/A-18 squadrons deployed, equating to an operations tempo (optempo) of greater then one-to-one, none of the three Marine Reserve F/A-18 squadrons have been activated.[3] Headquarters Marine Corps faces a critical choice: to mobilize the Reserve F/A-18 squadrons for use in the GWOT, to change their role, or to confront a possible loss of the Reserve Tactical Aviation force structure.

In September of 2004 the Marine Corps completed the decommissioning of VMFA-321, a 4th Marine Aircraft Wing Reserve F/A-18 squadron, as part of the Navy and Marine Corps' Tactical Aviation Integration (TAI) plan.[4] This decommissioning reduced the Marine Reserve F/A-18 force structure by 25%.[5] In light of the Department of Defense's push for transformation, and in the simple fact that not a single Marine Reserve F/A-18 squadron has been used in either the Global War on Terror (Operation Enduring Freedom / Operation Iraqi Freedom), Bosnia, or the Gulf War (Desert Shield / Desert Storm), the following question must be asked: Are the Marine Reserve F/A-18

---

[2] Tustin.

[3] Operations tempo (optempo) is defined as the rate at which units of the armed forces are involved in all military activities, including contingency operations, exercises, and training deployments. An optempo ratio of one-to-one would indicate a unit spent one day deployed for every one day that it was not deployed. For more information see Mark Brinkley, "The Way Ahead; After Iraq, top Marine sets a course for resetting the force and beyond," *Marine Corps Times*, 13 October 2003, 9.

[4] Tactical Aviation Integration (TAI) is agreement signed by the Navy and the Marine Corps to incorporate six additional Marine F/A-18 Squadrons (making a total of ten integrated Marine Hornet squadrons) into the Navy's Carrier Air Wings. For more information on this topic one can reference the United States Government Accountability Office Report to Congressional Committees, *Force Structure: Department of the Navy's Tactical Aviation Integration Plan is Reasonable, but Some Factors Could Affect Implementation*, GAO-04-900. (Washington, DC: Government Accountability Office, August 2004), 6. Cited hereafter as GAO-04-900 report to Congress.

[5] The decommissioning of VMFA-321 (as part of the TAI agreement) reduced the total number of Marine Corps Reserve F/A-18 squadrons from four down to three equating to a 25% loss in capability. For more information see GAO-04-900 report to Congress, 16.

squadrons relevant? If the answer to the question is that they are relevant, then why, to date, have these Reserve squadrons not been used in the Global War on Terror? What, if any, political, statutory, policy, or cultural issues need to be addressed to help provide the forcing function required for the Marine Corps leadership to make better use of the Reserve F/A-18 squadrons?

Or, on the other hand, if these squadrons are determined not to be relevant, what should the Marine Corps do with the remaining Reserve F/A-18 squadrons? Should they decommission them all and simply lose that capability in the Reserve structure, or should they change their role in some manner in order to provide a more needed capability? The latter could free up some needed force structure for low density, high demand capabilities required in countering emerging catastrophic, or disruptive threats that characterize the unconventional war American is fighting.[6] Either way, once the F/A-18 squadron relevancy question has been answered, the role that the remaining 4th Marine Aircraft Wing F/A-18 squadrons should play in the GWOT can be proposed.

To answer these questions, this paper will analyze the issues that influenced the Marine Corps decision makers' thought process when they elected not to mobilize a Reserve F/A-18 squadron for use in the GWOT. To this end, the author will look at the Marine Corps Reserves' mission, its policy, structure, and the role (if any) that the Reserve Tactical Aviation (TacAir) units have played in America's military history.[7] In doing so, many of the Reserve policies and cultural issues that shaped the Marine Corps decision makers' thought processes will be addressed. Armed with this information as

---

[6] Jason Shermen, "Rolling QDR Could Shape 05 Budget," *Defense News,* 6 December 2004, 1.
[7] TacAir is the commonly accepted abbreviation for Tactical Aviation. Though technically speaking Marine Corps Tactical Aviation includes all fixed wing aircraft, for the purpose of this paper the author will only be referring to the Reserve F/A-18 squadrons when using the TacAir abbreviation.

context, the author will attempt to determine what the future will look like for the Marine Reserve F/A-18 units. Then, potential courses of action and some recommendations will be provided which, if implemented, will help make better use of the Marine Corps Reserve F/A-18 squadrons, not only in today's war on terror, but in the future battles of tomorrow.

CHAPTER 1

"What began as a simple Air Force lightweight fighter prototype [the F/A-18 'Hornet'] has evolved into the most sophisticated warplane in the U.S. Navy and Marine Corps inventory."

--Dennis Jenkins
"The F/A-18 Hornet, A Navy Success Story"

"Relevant: Related to the matter at hand; pertinent."
"Pertinent: to pertain."
"Pertain: To be fitting or suitable."

--The American Heritage Dictionary
Second College Edition 2003

"We are all members of 'the first team.' We must all meet 'first team' standards."

--LtGen Dennis M. McCarthy, USMCR
Command General Marine Forces Reserve

ARE THE MARINE RESERVE F/A-18 SQUADRONS RELEVANT?

Are the Marine Reserve F/A-18 squadrons relevant? To answer the question, there must be a basic understanding of the following topics: the policy, statutory, and doctrinal guidelines that govern the use of the Reserve forces, the role in which the Marine Corps Reserve forces play in the military's total force construct, the current Reserve F/A-18 force structure, an evaluation of the military capabilities that these units can provide to the Combatant Commanders (CoComs), and any pertinent historical examples of previous uses of the Reserve F/A-18 units.[8] In addition, what missions, if any, are these units currently assigned by the CoComs, and if so, how do those assigned missions impact the answer to the relevancy question? Once an understanding of these

---

[8] Combatant Commanders (CoComs) are the military commanders whom are assigned a geographic area of responsibility by the President for fighting our nation's wars. For more information on these commands see Joint Publication, JP 0-2, *Unified Action Armed Forces (UNAAF),* (n.p., 10 July 2001), II-14.

topics is achieved, the reader will be able to conclude that the Reserve F/A-18 squadrons are in fact relevant.

RESERVE MOBILIZATION POLICY AND PROCEDURES

Title 10, section 262, of the United States Code, declares that the mission of the Reserve Forces is to provide trained and qualified units and individuals to be available for Active duty in time of war, national emergency, and at such times as national security may require.[9] This law provides the legal guidance and describes the requirements that must be satisfied to mobilize the Reserve forces of the U.S. military. First, the law states that in times of national emergency or war, the President of the United States can authorize the mobilization of the Reserves to fulfill the Active duty force requirements.[10] These mobilizations would, in theory, increase the number of Active military personnel up to a number that is assessed to be the required wartime end-strength to be able to complete the mission. There are five different statutes that legally quantify how many selected reservists can be mobilized and the time duration these reservists can be assigned to Active duty for each individual mobilization option (see figure #1 below).

---

[9] United States Code, Title 10, section 262, effective 2 January 2001.
[10] United States Code, Title 10, section 101, effective 2 January 2001.

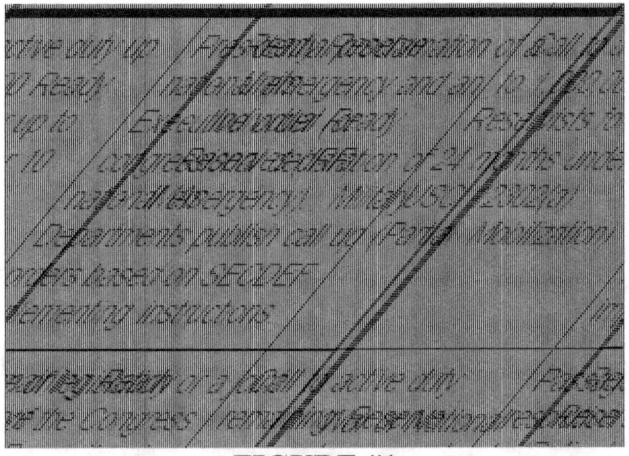

FIGURE #1
WAR OR NATIONAL EMERGENCY
RESERVE MOBILIZATION OPTIONS
JOINT PUBLICATION 4-05.1

Then, based on the Combatant Commander's assessment of his mission requirements produced in the Operation Plan (OPLAN), he requests the forces necessary to execute his plan and complete his mission.[11] The individual services are each responsible for preparing detailed mobilization plans to provide the Combatant Commander with the required forces needed to execute the OPLAN. These requests are vetted through the respective Service Chiefs who make the force recommendations to fulfill the requirement, and present them to the Chairman of the Joint Chiefs of Staff (CJCS). The CJCS, after close coordination with the Assistant Secretary of Defense and Reserve Affairs, advises the Secretary of Defense (SecDef) of the need to mobilize any Reserve forces to augment the Active force, and the timeframe for which those forces will be needed. If approved, the SecDef recommends the plan to the President, who will

---

[11] An OPLAN is the Combatant Commanders theater operational plan to achieve the strategic objectives in his area of responsibility. For more information see Joint Publication, JP 5-00.1, *Joint Doctrine for Campaign Planning,* (n.p., 25 January 2002), III 1-20.

then invoke the legal authority granted under Title 10 to order the mobilization of

Reserve forces to Active duty (see figure #2 below).[12]

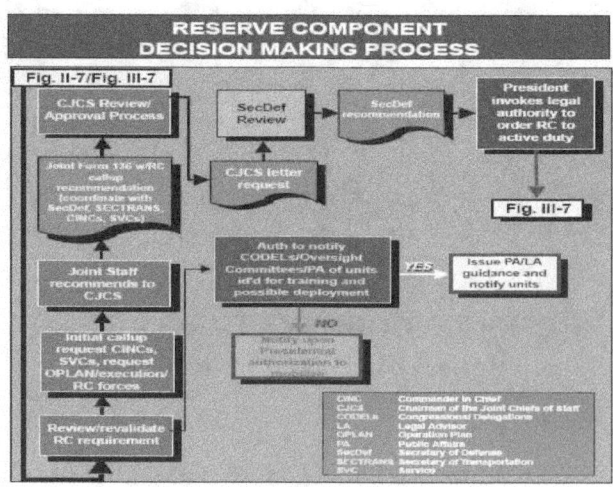

FIGURE #2
JOINT PUBLICATION 4-05.1

It is also important to understand the different service mobilization policies (see

figure #3 below) and the effect that these policies have on the activation process. What

are not stated in the policy are the philosophies by which the services train their

individual Reserve units in preparation for mobilization. The Marine Corps Reserve

units conduct their training plans with the idea that they will maintain a deployable

combat readiness at all times. If mobilized, the Marine units then require minimal time to

complete the required administrative processes to be ready to deploy. More times then

not the only delay in getting these forces into theatre are accrued from the lack of

available strategic movement capabilities.[13] This is a fundamental difference from the

Army's philosophy of first mobilizing their Reserve units, then providing a time period of

---

[12] Joint Publication, JP 4-05.1, *Reserve Component Decision Making Process*, (n.p., 11 November 1998), III-6, Figure III-4.

[13] MGen John W. Bergman, USMCR, Director, Reserve Affairs, HQMC, interview by the author, 6 December 2004. Cited hereafter as MGen Bergman interview.

some length for training and, once complete, then being ready to deploy at some significant time after they had been mobilized. In some cases these units require up to 270 days of training to be combat deployable.[14] There is an obvious impact to the amount of time that those units are available to the Combatant Commander when nearly half of the legally allotted time to be mobilized is used for training and readiness. The difference of philosophy has had a significant impact on the nation's forces and their availability for the CoCom to have the required assets required for completing his mission.

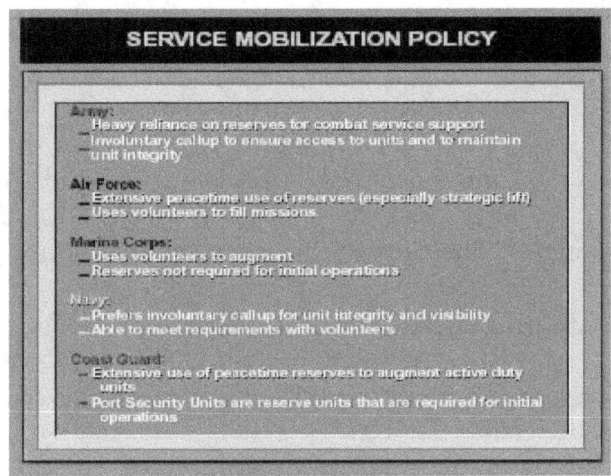

FIGURE #3
JOINT PUBLICATION 4-05.1

THE ROLE OF THE MARINE CORPS RESERVE IN TOTAL FORCE

The Nation's Total Force Policy was instituted in the 1970's during the Nixon administration under then Secretary of Defense Melvin R. Laird. In the aftermath of the Vietnam War, the political intent of the total force policy was to ensure that both Active and Reserve forces would be responsible for the nation's global security. This would, in effect, make sure that the political leaders would not be able to go to war without

---

[14] MGen Bergman interview.

mobilizing the American people through the use of their citizen soldiers, the Reserves. This was best summed up by Secretary Laird when he said that the total force was "a major step in which members of the National Guard and Reserve, instead of draftees, will be the initial and primary source of augmentation for the Active forces in any future emergency."[15] This was a significant change in America's national military strategy where the President would now be relying on the Reserve forces to augment and reinforce the Active duty force, versus fulfilling those requirements through a selective service draft process.

The Marine Corps' total force policy is one that stems from the nation's total force policy. The Marine's total force consists of an Active Component (AC) of about 178,000 Marines, a Reserve Component (RC) of nearly 100,000 Reserve Marines, and numerous retired personnel.[16] The Corps primary obligation to the American people is to provide a combat ready Marine Air Ground Task Force (MAGTF), the nation's expeditionary force-in-readiness, that can respond to a crisis anyplace in the world. The Marine Corps Reserve plays a vital role in the Marine Corps' total force policy by providing the Active duty with trained units and qualified individuals to reinforce and augment the Active component during times of war, national emergencies, and other times which national security may require.[17] Currently, the Marine Corps Reserve, organized under the Commander Marine Forces Reserve (COMMARFORRES), makes up nearly 23% of the Marine Corps Total Force. The Marine Corps Mobilization Management Plan (MPLAN) provides the details and appropriate guidance to the

---

[15] Major Daniel P. Coombs, USMC, Command and Staff College Masters Thesis Paper. *Reserve Integration: A Corps Competency.* Quantico, VA: Gray Research Center, 2003, 6.

[16] MGen Bergman interview.

[17] Marine Corps Doctrinal Publication, MCDP 1-0, *Marine Corps Operations*, (n.p., September 2001), 1-16. Cited hereafter as MCDP 1-0.

contingency planners for mobilizing or recalling the members of the Marine Corps

Reserve in order to fulfill the required mission.[18]

THE CURRENT RESERVE F/A-18 FORCE STRUCTURE

In owning all of the Marine Corps Reserve Forces, COMMARFORRES is

responsible for making sure all of his forces are trained and ready to mobilize when

called upon by the President of the United States (POTUS) and the American people.

The same division, wing, and combat service support concept that the Active component

uses, also is applied to the Reserve component.[19] Under this concept,

COMMARFORRES, owns the 4th Marine Division, the 4th Marine Aircraft Wing, and a

Force Service Support Group (FSSG). This structure closely mirrors that of the Active

duty component in force structure, capabilities and equipment.[20] Currently, the 4th

Marine Aircraft Wing (4th MAW) contains three F/A-18 "Hornet" squadrons.

As of September 2004, the Marine Corps Reserves went from having four

squadrons down to three, reducing the Reserve total force contribution of single seat F/A-

18's down to 27% (see figure #4 below). The remaining three squadrons include:

VMFA-112, stationed at the Joint Reserve Base (JRB) in Fort-Worth, Texas, under

Marine Aircraft Group forty-one (MAG-41); VMFA-134, stationed at Marine Corps Air

Station Miramar, California, under MAG-46; and VMFA-142, stationed at Dobbins, Joint

Reserve Base in Atlanta, Georgia, under MAG-42. Each of these squadrons are assigned

---

[18] Marine Corps Reserve Guidebook, Section V, Paragraph 1. *Manpower and Reserve Affairs Home Page*, https://Inweb1.manpower.usmc.mil, web page URL "http://mcrsc.mfr.usmc.mil/Guidebook/Guidbook.asp," accessed 27 December 2004.

[19] The Active duty Marine Corps by law is organized into three Marine Divisions, three Marine Aircraft Wings, and three Force Service Support Groups. For more information see MCDP 1-0, 1-2.

[20] For more information see the MFR command relationships wire diagram in MCDP 1-0, 1-5.

twelve F/A-18 fighter-attack aircraft, of which all have, or will be undergoing

Engineering Change Proposal number 583 (ECP-583), which upgrades the aircraft's

radar, avionics, data-link, and weapons delivery capabilities.[21] Of note, unlike the Active

component, each of these squadrons is based at different geographical locations. There

are a variety of reasons for this, all of which are inherent to the Reserve construct.

Additionally, each of these squadrons are assigned to a different higher headquarters,

which include no other like type-model aircraft. These points will be discussed further in

subsequent chapters.

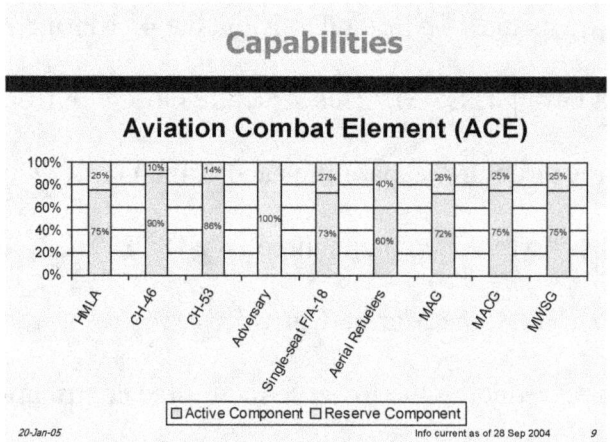

FIGURE #4
RESERVE CONTRIBUTION TO TOTAL FORCE
% SINGLE-SEAT F/A-18 CAPABILITY

---

[21] ECP-583 is an engineering change proposal that significantly upgrades the capability of the F/A-18 aircraft. This change is approved and funded and is due to be complete by 2005. The changes included a better radar (APG-73), improved avionics, GPS and precision-guided weapon delivery capabilities, digital close air support capability, a Link-16 data link, and numerous other enhancements. For more information on ECP-583 see *Jane's: All the Worlds Aircraft 2001-2002*, ed. Paul Jackson and others (Surrey, UK: Sentinel House, 2002), 577.

WHAT CAPABILITIES DO THE RESERVE F/A-18 SQUADRONS PROVIDE?

The Reserve F/A-18 squadron's mission is to provide combat capable airplanes and pilots to perform a wide variety of mission tasks in support of the MAGTF Commander.[22] These essential tasks are derived from the assigned capabilities inherent in the mission essential task lists (METL's) that are listed in the Marine Corps F/A-18 Training and Readiness Manual (T&R). These METL's include a variety of fighter and attack profiles such as deep air strikes, air interdiction, combat air patrols, ground close air support, armed reconnaissance, and the suppression of the enemy air defenses.[23] Additionally, it is important to point out that both the AC and RC squadrons are assigned the same mission, perform the same tasks, and it can be argued that when the reservists are current, their tactical execution of these essential tasks are superior to that of their Active counterparts.

There are four contributors that enable Reserve pilots to achieve such an enhanced performance and mission success when they are called upon to execute. First, all Marine Reserve F/A-18 pilots have been raised through the same pipeline as the Active duty pilots. They all have completed Officer Candidate School, The Basic School, and then Flight School to become Naval Aviators who fly the F/A-18 Hornet. So, the mindset and ethos of Reserve Marine Aviators are the same as those Active duty pilots, and that is "to support the Marine rifleman."

---

[22] Training and Education Command, United States Marine Corps, *F/A-18 Training and Readiness Manual (T&R), MCO 3500.46,* 10 September 2004. *Marine Corps Training and Education Command Home Page,* www.tecom.usmc.mil, web page URL: www.usmc.mil/directivnsf/mco?, accessed 05 January 2005. Hereafter cited as F/A-18 T&R Manual, MCO 3500.46.

[23] For more information about these missions and any specific F/A-18 METLs see the F/A-18 T&R Manual, MCO 3500.46.

Second, all the Reserve pilots have had at least one Active duty tour before they decided to leave the Active component and join the Reserves. Based on flight hours alone, the experience level of the typical Reserve F/A-18 pilot is twice that of the average Active duty fleet Hornet pilot.[24] A typical reservist has 2000 flight hours and commensurate instructor qualifications. The average first tour Hornet pilot has something less then 1000 flight hours and only a few, if any, instructor qualifications.[25] The amount of Reserve pilot experience is magnified when one considers the fact that the majority of these pilots have had previous combat experience while on Active duty.

In addition to an extraordinary amount of expertise, the Reserve squadrons enjoy a unit cohesion that is without peer.[26] This cohesiveness stems from the personnel continuity and shared origins that contribute to strong personal relationships within the squadrons. The trust and confidence that these relationships provide, creates a unit that is bonded together in all the ways needed to fight effectively and to be able to deal with the psychological stresses associated with combat operations.

The training and readiness of the Reserve units is the final contributor affecting their ability to perform at such a high level of mission effectiveness. There is no separate Training and Readiness (T&R) manual for the Reserve F/A-18 squadrons. The commander is responsible for ensuring his squadron is trained and ready to deploy. The squadron must be combat ready to perform the entire list of mission essential tasks listed

---

[24] MGen Bergman interview.

[25] The average Reserve F/A-18 pilot has 2000 flight hours, and the following qualifications: mission commander, division leader, section leader, Air Combat Tactics Instructor and an advanced fighter weapons school qualification from either Top Gun, or the MAWTS-1 Weapons and Tactics Course. The average first tour Active duty F/A-18 pilot has less then 1000 flight hours, and the following qualifications: division or section leader and a combat wingman qualification. Colonel William Blalock, USMCR, Deputy Commander MAG-41, JRB Fort-Worth, Texas, interview by the author, 10 January 2005. Cited hereafter as Col Blalock interview.

[26] Cohesion is defined as "the bonding together of members of a unit or organization in such a way as to sustain their will and commitment to each other, their unit, and the mission."

in the T&R manual. Although it is hard for the Reserve squadron's pilots to maintain

their currency, they do maintain proficiency.[27] The Reserve pilots rely upon their

extensive experience to turn their proficiency into mission currency when they mobilize.

This is practiced annually during each Reserve squadron's required two week Active

training period.

Couple the improved capabilities that ECP-583 provides to the F/A-18, with the

intrinsic pilot experience and unit cohesion of the Reserve squadrons, the resulting

capability is more then a suitable asset for the CoComs to accomplish their fighter-attack

missions. Therefore; one can conclude, the Reserve F/A-18 squadrons are indeed a

suitable asset for providing the mission essential tasks any CoCom would require of a

strike-fighter unit.

HISTORY OF MARINE RESERVE F/A-18 SQUADRONS IN COMBAT

The mission of the Marine Corps Reserve is to provide trained units or individuals

to reinforce or augment the Active force. To date, the Reserve F/A-18 squadrons have

not been used in any contingency or wartime combat operation since the introduction of

the F/A-18 aircraft into the Reserve structure in 1991.[28] This is by no means the

precedent; in fact, Marine Reserve fighter and attack aircraft have been used in many of

---

[27] The T&R manual defines currency as "a control measure used to provide an additional margin of safety based on exposure frequency to a particular skill set." Proficiency is "a measure of achievement of a specific skill set." Refly factors establish the maximum time allowed between the demonstration of those particular skills. Reserve pilots maintain individual proficiency, but often times drop out of currency.

[28] United States Marine Corps, Marine Forces Reserve. *History of VMFA-321*. *Marine Forces Reserve Home Page*, www.mfr.usmc.mil, web page URL http://www.mfr.usmc.mil/4thmaw/mag49/vmfa321, accessed 13 October 2004.

our nation's wars. The most recent conflict in which Reserve fixed wing fighter attack aircraft were mobilized was for use in the Korean War in 1950.[29]

WHAT DO THESE RESERVE F/A-18 ASSETS PROVIDE THE NATION?

In the most recent years, the Marine Corps Reserve units have not only been ready to augment or reinforce the Active duty forces, but they also have been increasingly called upon to conduct peacetime operational support. This type of support enhances readiness throughout the Marine Corps total force structure by reducing the operational strain placed on the Active duty forces and increasing deployment flexibility. The Reserve F/A-18 units are no different. Although they have not been activated for any of the most recent wars since 1991, their role has been to provide the nation with peacetime operational support for the Active duty squadrons.

Additionally, since the Navy and Marine Corps' agreement to integrate the services tactical aviation assets, all of the Reserve F/A-18 squadrons have been implemented into the existing numbered OPLANS.[30] This fact in and of itself makes these TacAir assets pertinent to the Marine Corps' total force structure.

---

[29] All the historical combat uses of the Reserve fixed wing aircraft can be found in Peter Mersky's book titled "U.S. Marine Corps Aviation, 1912 to the Present." Though beyond the scope of this paper, in short the Reserve fixed wing aviation was used in WWI, WWII, and Korea, with no activations for Vietnam, Desert Storm, Bosnia or the current GWOT.

[30] The specific numbered war plan and its respective geographical Combatant Commander is classified, but the Reserve F/A-18 squadrons are force listed on various OPLANS. LtCol David Hitchcock, USMC, Aviation Plans and Policy, TacAir Plans, Headquarters Marine Corps, Washington, DC, interview by the author, 22 September 2004. Cited hereafter as LtCol Hitchcock interview.

THE BOTTOM LINE: THE F/A-18 UNITS ARE RELEVANT, YET UNUSED

From the above analysis the following conclusions can be drawn: First, the Reserve F/A-18 squadrons are indeed relevant. They are more then suitable for providing the required fighter attack missions, and they are pertinent in that they are listed as required forces for supporting the Combatant Commanders numbered war plans. Additionally, they remain ready, willing, and able to be tested as vital members of the nation's total force construct.

Yet, when the time came to flow the forces into the Time-Phased Force and Deployment Data (TPFDD) for Operation Iraqi Freedom (OIF), the Marine Reserve F/A-18 squadrons were left out.[31] The following chapter will address the reasons why the author believes the Reserve Hornets were not allocated to the Combatant Commander and, therefore, not mobilized for the GWOT.

---

[31] The TPFDD is the document that flows the forces that Secretary of Defenses has approved and allocated to the CoCom for operations in his geographical area of responsibility. For more information see Joint Publication, JP 5-00.1, *Joint Doctrine for Campaign Planning,* (n.p., 25 January 2002), III 3-17.

CHAPTER #2

> *"The Reserve Component; left to its own devices the Reserve Component will not optimize its training and readiness to augment and reinforce the Active Component."*
>
> *"The Active Component; left to its own devices the Active Component will destroy or decimate its Reserve Component."*
>
> *"The American People; left to their own devices the American people without the Reserve Component will lose touch with the Military as a whole."*
>
> *--MGen Bergman*
> *Director of Manpower and Reserve Affairs*
>
>
> *"The last thing I want to do is break the Reserves, we're not close to that now. But, that's a constant thought in my mind."*
>
> *--General Mike Hagee*
> *33rd Commandant of the Marine Corps*

WHY WERE'NT RESERVE F/A-18 UNITS ACTIVATED FOR THE GWOT?

Since it has been concluded in chapter one that the Reserve F/A-18 squadrons have a relevant capability, then, why did the Marine Corps leadership decide not to mobilize a Reserve F/A-18 squadron for use in Operation Iraqi Freedom? There is no one single explanation to answer this question; in fact, there are many reasons that affected this decision, each of which is complicated to say the least. But, if one had to summarize why the Reserve F/A-18 squadrons were not mobilized, the answer could be explained best like this: "It was a combination of politics, policy, and service culture."[32]

The following paragraphs will discuss all three of the issues as they relate to the decision not to mobilize the Reserve hornets, and, in the broader context, regarding the mobilization of the Reserve forces in general. The author, having not been present when

---

[32] LtCol Hitchcock interview.

this decision was made, does not claim to know all the issues involved, nor the logic behind each of these issues' agendas. But, based on the interviews conducted, one can draw some fairly concrete conclusions as to what the mindset was and, therefore, the reasons why the decision was made not to activate a Reserve F/A-18 squadron for use in Operation Iraqi Freedom.

POLITICAL, STATUTORY, POLICY, and CULTURAL ISSUES

There are numerous political, statutory and cultural issues germane to RC mobilization, which when combined seem to constrain the Marine Corps leadership's decision making ability. This is especially true when leaders make decisions that involve the activation of Reserve Component forces. The greater the knowledge and understanding these decision makers have regarding the RC mobilization restraints, then the better these types of decisions will be. If the decision makers can masterfully balance the issues while using all of the available assets, then the impacts upon both the RC and AC will be mitigated, and the Marine Corps as a whole can realize the maximum gains that total force readiness provides.

Under current law, in a time of war or national emergency, the President of the United States can authorize his legislative authority under title 10 of the U.S. code to involuntarily mobilize Reserve forces to Active duty, therefore, bringing the armed forces of the United States to a state of readiness required to prosecute the war. The partial mobilization authorization, which was signed by the President in September 2001, gave the U.S. Service Chiefs the decision-making authority via the Secretary of Defense, to mobilize the Reserve forces they deemed necessary to prosecute the Global War on

Terror.[33] A partial mobilization decision by the President authorizes the activation of up to 1,000,000 ready Reserves for a time period of no more then 2 years (see figure #1 on page 7).

With the Presidential authorization in place, the Service Chiefs had to make the force allocation decisions based on the CoComs OPLAN requirements. When making important decisions regarding Reserve force mobilization, the Marine Corps leadership, likened to any large institution's leadership, had to consider and balance many different factors. This is especially true when such decisions affect an entire institution.[34] The Marine Corps is no different. In fact, it may be worse, because military Service Chiefs must answer to the larger parental bureaucracy of the Department of Defense. The current Secretary of Defense questioned every single force recommendation to ensure that it was required and justifiable to the President before he approved it.[35] In an attempt to understand the logic and reasoning behind why the decision was made the way it was, one must first understand the context of the environment in which the decision was made. Once the time, place, and circumstance of that environment is understood, then one can draw some conclusions as to why the Reserve F/A-18 squadrons were not activated.

The force requirements and allocation decisions for Operation Iraqi Freedom were being made during the fall of 2002. The deliberate planning process yielded a Reserve F/A-18 squadron being apportioned to the TPFDD for the OPLAN. But, the SecDef decided to use a request for forces process, rather then simply approving the TPFDD, as

---

[33] U. S. President, Executive Order 13223, "President Orders Ready Reserve of Armed Forces to Active Duty," 14 September 2001. Cited hereafter as U.S. President EO 13223, 14 September 2001.

[34] LtGen James F. Amos, USMC, Commanding General II MEF, telephone interview by the author, 3 December 2004. Cited hereafter as LtGen Amos telephone interview.

[35] Colonel Mantford C. Hawkins, USMC, Commanding Officer MAG-41, JRB Fort-Worth, TX, telephone interview by the author, 8 December 2004. Cited hereafter as Col Hawkins telephone interview.

it was originally planned. This resulted in the Reserve F/A-18 squadron being replaced with an Active duty squadron and therefore no Reserve TacAir squadrons would be allocated to U.S. Central Command for use in OIF. [36] The first factor that influenced this decision stems from the Marine Corps service mobilization policy. The Marine Corps' policy dictates that the service does not require Reserve forces for initial operations, which is contrary to the Army and Air Force policies. But, having a Reserve Squadron already apportioned on the original plan, and the presidential authorization in place, the decision not to follow this policy could have been made without too much scrutiny.

The second factor involved in influencing this Marine Corps decision centered on a shortsighted political assumption. At the time when these force requirements and allocation decisions were being made by the Marine leadership, the Department of Defense was making the assumption that Operation Iraqi Freedom would be a very short-lived war. They believed that after the quick defeat of Saddam's regime, the management of the country would be handed off to the exiles led by the Iraqi exile Ahmad Chalabi. [37] Thus a short commitment of something less then a year's time, would allow the Active component to be able to handle all of the Marine TacAir requirements without the help from the Reserves. The short war, quick turnover to the Iraqi National Committee assumption turned out to be not only shortsighted, but also very wrong. [38]

The final issue that played a key factor in the leadership's decision not to mobilize a Reserve squadron is the institutional culture and biases that exist within the Marine

---

[36] Col Hawkins telephone interview.

[37] George Parker, "Letter From Baghdad, War after War," *The New Yorker Magazine*, 24 November 2003, 50-58.

[38] Numerous books and articles have been written about the Penagon's perceived failure to properly plan for the security and stability phase of Iraqi Freedom, but this topic is beyond the scope of this paper. The important point is the outcome, a much longer commitment in Iraqi, which is relevant to this paper.

Corps. Military culture is the set of attitudes, values, and beliefs of the leaders that influence and/or make the decisions. The first cultural issue lies between the Active and Reserve components. A common attitude found among Active duty Marines is that their Reserve component counterparts are not first team players, and, for the most part, are just quitters looking for a job.[39] This attitude and cultural bias results from a fundamental lack of understanding of the Reserve component and the warfighting capability it provides to the Marine Corps.

Second, the Marine Corps as a service has always had the belief of institutional paranoia. This stems from the Marine Corps' constant battle for their existence throughout its 229-year history.[40] Having this mindset, the Marine Corps has always tried to accomplish more with less, and, therefore, do what Marines do best, improvise, adapt, and overcome. However, more often then not, this frame of mind tends to lead to a shortsighted decision that ends up as a detriment to the individual Marines who ultimately have to carry the load. This is manifested today in the unit optempo ratios being at 1-to-1 or greater throughout the Marine Corps.[41]

Third, there was a cultural fear of breaking the Marine Reserve force, a perceived cultural fear of potential internal strife; Active duty personnel problems, the potential internal infighting that could arise from sending a Reserve unit to war instead of an Active unit, and the fear of what the political backlash may have been in light of this

---

[39] This attitude comes from many Inspector and Instructor (I&I) staff Marines who report quotable quotes from Reserve unit bulletin boards such as "I've quite once, I'll do it again," and "That's your job, this is my hobby." Major Don Roach, USMC, Inspector and Instructor staff, VMFA-321, 4th Marine Aircraft Wing, Andrews AFB, MD, interview by the author 30 September 2004.

[40] Although beyond the scope of this paper, the Marine Corps as an institution has fought for its very existence after WWI, WWII, Korea, and Vietnam. For more information see Robert Worley's manuscript, "*Marine Corps*," (undated manuscript draft) pages 1-35, MAGTF Organizations, USMC Command and Staff College Syllabus AY 2004-05.

[41] MGen Timothy F. Ghormley, USMC, Director, Manpower Plans and Policy Division, HQMC, Quantico, VA, interview by the author, 6 December 2004. Cited hereafter as MGen Ghormley interview.

mobilization decision. What kind of message would this decision be sending to the civilian leadership regarding the Marine Corps as an institution? The sum of these feared outcomes outweighed the added value of asking to mobilize a Reserve squadron. The risk analysis led to the Marine leaders making the easy, short-term decision not to activate the Reserve F/A-18 squadrons, instead of the harder long-term decision for the overall Marine Corps.

THE BOTTOM LINE: THE REASON IS A COMPLICATED MIX OF ISSUES

From the above analysis, the reason why the Reserve F/A-18 squadrons were not activated for use in Operation Iraqi Freedom is complicated and is best summarized as a combination of reasons stemming from mobilization policy, politics, and service culture. The combined by-product of these issues equated to an over-arching fear to mobilize these resources. One could argue that at the time when the decision was made not to use the Reserve F/A-18 squadrons, the Department of Defense was assuming Iraqi Freedom would be soon achieved, thus allowing the Active component to handle all of the Marine TacAir requirements. This assumption, though valid at the time, turned out to be very wrong. When one combines this political influence, with the no initial Reserve force requirement policy, and the inherent Marine Corps cultural issues, the result produced a shortsighted decision made from bad assumptions. The time is now to look long range and mobilize the Reserve F/A-18 squadrons.

Now that there is a basic understanding of the Reserve F/A-18 squadron's capabilities, their structure, and the mobilization issues, the reader will be better equipped to discern the author's logic and reasoning behind the following potential courses of action. If the Marine Corps leadership decides to embrace these recommendations, the resulting effect will be seen in the enhanced use of the Reserve F/A-18 squadrons.

CHAPTER #3

> *"Course of Action: a viable solution to a problem which lies in the realm of possibilities presented to the commander for a decision."*
>
> *--Joint Publication 1-02*
>
> *"The development of the possible courses of action requires that they be a specific, measurable, action which is realistic, relevant and time limited."*
>
> *--MCWP 5-1, The Marine Corps Planning Process*
>
> *"Reserve assets [specifically Marine Reserve F/A-18's] that had not been decommissioned must be optimized for integration in future combat roles."*
>
> *--GAO 'Force Structure' Report to Congress*
> *GAO-04-900, August 2004*

POSSIBLE COURSES OF ACTION (COA's)

In light of the issues discussed in the previous chapters, one must look ahead and ask; what does the future look like, not only for the Reserve F/A-18 squadrons, but the Reserves as a whole? The Marine Corps' Active duty components have a finite number of resources available and they are currently being stretched very thin; therefore, the Reserve F/A-18 squadrons should be used.[42] In doing so, they will be providing real op-temp relief for the Active duty, while additionally ensuring that Reserve TacAir remains relevant into the foreseeable future.

The following paragraphs will offer the Marine Corps' leadership five possible courses of action to determine the Reserve F/A-18 squadron's future plight. The first one provides an immediate solution for making better use of the Marine Corps Reserve F/A-18 units to support the GWOT. The second, third, and fourth courses of action provide

---

[42] MGen Ghormley interview.

options for the future, which if implemented, can increase the Marine Corps' overall total force warfighting capability. The final course of action portrays the potential outcome of the Reserve TacAir aircraft, if the decision is made to maintain the status quo. The author does not claim that these are the only options available to help fix this problem, yet they do provide a range of possibilities that address the issue not only for today, but also for the future to come.

> *"With regard to the Reserves [in the context of the Global War on Terror], we have to do what is best for the institution, we can't afford to have forces sitting on the shelf."*
>
> *--LtGen James F. Amos, USMC*
> *Commanding General II MEF*

COA #1: MOBILIZE 4TH MAW F/A-18 SQUADRONS FOR USE IN THE GWOT

The first option is the recommended course of action that the Marine Corps leadership should follow. This option recommends the mobilization of the 4th MAW F/A-18 squadrons for use in the Global War on Terror. By doing so, the Reserve units would help today's Marine Corps total force by reducing the operational tempo of the Active duty F/A-18D's by almost 50% over the next 3 years.[43]

The situation in Iraq continues to dictate a requirement for a U.S. military presence, currently including a Tactical Aviation obligation, and there is no evidence to suggest that this requirement is going to change anytime soon.[44] Additionally, this operation is not the only commitment that requires Marine TacAir assets. Therefore, the

---

[43] LtCol Hitchcock interview.
[44] Colonel Robert Brady, USMC, Director, Aviation Plans and Policy, Headquarters Marine Corps, Washington, DC, interview by the author, 1 December 2004. Cited hereafter as Col Brady interview.

Marine Corps' decision makers must determine what the total number of TacAir requirements are, and based on those commitments, make a well informed decision whether or not to use the Marine Reserve Hornets in OIF. If they do, the decision makers will determine that effective 01 January 2005 the Commandant of the Marine Corps' is greater then 100% committed with regard to his Active duty TacAir assets.[45] With the Commandant's Active force working at nearly a 1-to-1 optempo ratio, the decision to mobilize the Reserve Hornets would reduce this stress on the Active component.[46]

The Presidential partial mobilization authorization that is currently in place allows individual reservist to be involuntarily mobilized for up to two years.[47] Therefore, to maximize the amount of relief that the Reserves can provide to the Active component, the recommendation is to activate two of 4th MAW's F/A-18 squadrons, each for a two-year period. With current OIF rotations lasting seven months, a two-year mobilization effectively allows each squadron to be able to mobilize, complete two seven-month OIF rotations, and then demobilize within the current statute's two-year legal limit. This plan would provide Reserve coverage of four, seven-month OIF rotations, therefore significantly reducing the Active duty TacAir operations-tempo.

The time to act upon this plan is not an endless proposition. As previously determined in chapter one, the experience level of the Reserve F/A-18 pilots is arguably twice that of their Active duty counterparts. But, the longer the Reserve Hornet squadrons go without being mobilized for the GWOT, the more that experience base will shift back towards favoring the Active duty forces. Within the next two to three years, most all of the Active duty F/A-18 pilots will have flown in combat in either OIF or OEF,

---

[45] LtCol Hitchcock interview.
[46] Col Brady interview.
[47] U.S. President EO 13223, 14 September 2001.

while the Reserves remain on the sideline. This will reduce what 4th MAW considers to be its critical capability, their experience, and, therefore, fundamentally threatens their existence all together.[48]

As the GWOT continues, any existing Reserve units that have not participated in sharing the load will soon come under a tremendous amount of budgetary scrutiny. We will eventually have to face the reality that money being spent on a force structure that has never been used may not be needed, especially at a time when labor is in such demand for the war on terror. To prevent this from happening, the Reserve F/A-18 squadrons need to be put into play and used for the GWOT.

Its been previously determined that the Marine Reserve F/A-18 units are relevant. They provide the same, if not an enhanced, combat capability to the nation's Combatant Commanders, and the Presidential mobilization authorization has already been approved. The only remaining requirement would be for the Commandant to request their mobilization through the Secretary of Defense. Yet, if this problem is not addressed, the fact will remain that these forces are, and will continue to be under utilized. This vary lack of use could lead to their eventual demise. It's hard for the Reserve F/A-18 units to assist the Combatant Commander in accomplishing his mission when they are sitting at home on the shelf. The time is upon us for the Marine leadership to act decisively and mobilize the Reserve Hornets.

---

[48] Col Hawkins telephone interview.

> *"Reserve Component (RC) forces are an integral part of the USMC total force. USMC RC forces are incorporated in the UDP, MEU rotations, and unscheduled MAGTF commitments via modifications to this schedule and/or appropriate orders. Activation of USMC RC forces to be coordinated with CMC, CDRUSJFCOM, COMMARFORLANT, and COMMARFORRES as authorized by appropriate authority."*
>
> MCBUL 3120 (FY 04-07)

COA #2: MOBILIZE 4TH MAW F/A-18 SQUADRONS FOR UDP RELIEF

The second course of action is to mobilize 4th MAW F/A-18 squadrons for use in Iwakuni, Japan, for Active duty optempo relief by providing force presence operations as part of the Marine Corps' unit deployment program (UDP). This, like COA #1, would significantly reduce the operations tempo of the Active duty forces by reducing the total number of TacAir commitments the Active component must fill. This usage also solves the desired second order effect, which is to maintain the Reserve TacAir relevance.

This option was proved viable when Marine Forces Reserve sent VMFA-112 to the Western Pacific in June of 2004. The squadron volunteered to be mobilized for 90 days in order to provide optempo relief for active duty forces assigned to the III Marine Expeditionary Force (MEF). By reinforcing the U.S. military presence mission in Asia, other III MEF forces were allowed to deploy to OIF. Although not directly replacing an Active duty VMFA squadron in a UDP rotation, the concept is much the same and was proven successful. Many important learning points from VMFA-112's deployment would be instrumental in making this course-of-action a practical solution.[49]

To complete this option, each of the three Reserve F/A-18 squadrons could be mobilized for an eight month time period. By doing so, it would provide each unit about

---

[49] W. G. Ford, "Cowboys Tame the Far East: VMFA-112," *Leatherneck*, Vol 87., Issue 10, October 2004, 26-28.

a month on either side of the normal six-month UDP cycle for training and administrative requirements. Then, by staggering each of these squadron mobilization dates by six months, there would be enough of an overlap to provide all three squadrons with the same requirements while providing the Active component with three UDP cycles of relief. This plan can have numerous branches or sequels depending on the desired amount of Active component relief that's required to be gained.

The problem with this COA resides in the legal and political realm.[50] There would have to be changes to the language in the laws and policies that govern the use of Reserve forces. Most Reserve entitlements are tied to contingency operations. Could a UDP be considered part of a contingency, if that Reserve unit were mobilized to provide Active duty deployment relief stemming from wartime requirements? It's unlikely.[51] Therefore, without a Title 10 language change, effectively making all the Reserve member entitlements the same, whether they volunteered or were mobilized, it's doubtful that this option would carry a whole lot of weight if proposed to the SecDef.[52]

Under the current law, this COA may not be the best option, but it is definitely a viable option for the future. Title 10 of the U.S. Code would require some legal work in order for the lawyers to be able to recommend the proper language changes required to make this option possible.

---

[50] Col Hawkins telephone interview.

[51] In the 2 February 2005 GAO-05-285T "Military Personnel" report to Congress, it was recommended that DOD develop a strategic framework that sets human capital goals concerning the availability of its reserve force to meet the longer-term requirements of the GWOT, and that DOD identify policies that should be linked within the strategic framework. For more information on this topic one can reference the United States Government Accountability Office Report to Congressional Committees, *Military Personnel: A Strategic Approach is Needed to Address Long-term Guard and Reserve Force Availability*, GAO-05-285T. (Washington, DC: Government Accountability Office, 2 February 2005), 17.

[52] Col Blalock interview.

COA #3:   MOVE ALL THREE SQUADRONS TO JRB FORT-WORTH, TEXAS

The third option is one that would look toward the future to provide the Marine Corps with an improved warfighting capability, while simultaneously transforming the Reserve F/A-18 structure in the process. This option ensures that the Reserve F/A-18's remain relevant, reduces the fiscal cost and overhead, and improves safety and oversight, all the while increasing the overall warfighting capability of the Marine Corps.

The plan would entail moving the two remaining Reserve squadrons (VMFA-134, and VMFA-142 based in Miramar, CA, and Atlanta's Dobbins JRB, in GA) to the Joint Reserve Base in Fort-Worth, TX, thus co-locating all three Reserve F/A-18 squadrons together. This would also bring all three squadrons under the same higher headquarters, namely Marine Aircraft Group forty-one (MAG-41), which is historically commanded by an Active duty F/A-18 or C-130 pilot. By co-locating the squadrons with their Reserve intermediate level maintenance and logistics squadron (MALS-41) it would optimize their organizational effectiveness.[53]

Once all three squadrons are co-located, maintaining the Reserve Hornet relevancy would become very easy and could be done without having to rely on the fact that each squadron is force listed on an OPLAN. With all three squadrons co-located, the

---

[53] Marine Aviation Logistics Support Squadron forty-one (MALS-41) is the intermediate level maintenance and parts supply point for the Reserve Hornet squadrons.

capability would exist to routinely source a six-month, ten to twelve aircraft deployment once every two years, for use in either a contingency operation or UDP requirement. Additionally, the capability could exist to source a four to six plane deployment with little or no pre-notice requirement. This type of capability could be used to support any pop-up higher headquarters type missions, or any Joint or Marine Corps exercise that requires a F/A-18 capability.

With all three squadrons located at the same base, there could be significant savings in logistics and overhead. For instance, aircraft maintenance and part supply costs would be reduced simply because they would be co-located with their intermediate level maintenance and supply squadron. This is currently not the case at Miramar or the JRB in Atlanta. Additionally, the JRB in Fort-Worth has the requisite hangar and ramp space required for the additional airplanes and the basing requirements for the Marines.[54]

Once co-located, the MAG-41 Commanding Officer could combine the squadron's daily aircraft maintenance effort. The synergy gained from doing this would allow for significant improvements in aircraft maintenance quality, increase oversight, improve safety, and gain the potential to reduce the overall manning requirements. With the improvement of the maintenance alone, comes improved aircraft availability for training and deployments. This increased capability would enhance pilot training and readiness levels and afford the opportunity to concentrate on a robust training plan for the squadrons. Combining all of the improvements provided in this COA results in an increased overall warfighting capability and a relevant, dynamic, flexible Active duty operations relief potential for the Marine Corps total force structure.

---

[54] Col Hawkins telephone interview.

There are two disadvantages to this option. The first is the Reserve

demographics. The Marine Reserve leadership will be quick to argue two points why this

may not work demographically.[55] First, they would say that there would not be enough

Marines in the Fort-Worth area to source this increased requirement. Then they would

add, that by moving the squadrons, the Marine Corps would be giving up its ties in the

local communities. In theory, both are valid points, but the fact remains both Atlanta and

San Diego would still have Reserve Marines located at their respective bases to provide

the community out reach, and the Dallas-Fort-Worth area has a large enough population

base to draw the required personnel numbers.

The second push back item that the Reserve leadership would point out involves

the politics that are inherently obvious when moving a Reserve squadron from one state

to another. This may be true when dealing with VMFA-142 in Atlanta, but would not

seem to be the case for San Diego. Either way, if these decisions are tied into the Base

Realignment and Closure process, there may be some maneuver room to allow for such

moves.[56] Although the political ramifications to this option may pose a significant

roadblock to the ability of selecting this COA, the gains in efficiency still outweigh the

risks of potential reprisal by significantly increasing the warfighting capability of the

Reserve Hornets. Therefore, in keeping with the transformation mindset, this option for

the future certainly warrants additional consideration and study at a minimum.

---

[55] Col Blalock interview.
[56] The Base Realignment and Closure (BRAC) process is set to begin in 2005. It has been
suggested that both the Dobbins JRB in Atlanta, GA and Marine Corps Air Station Miramar, CA are on the
list of bases to be considered by the BRAC commission.

> *"We should take a very hard look at those units that were not used during Desert Shield/Desert Storm, that were not used in operations Enduring Freedom and Iraqi Freedom, or during the 90's as operational tempo relief, and ask ourselves the hard question: 'Are they necessary and what would be more relevant and useful if they aren't necessary?'"*
>
> *--MGen Arnold L. Punaro, USMCR (Ret)*
> *Former Director, Reserve Affairs*

COA #4: DECOMMISSION THE REMAINING F/A-18 SQUADRONS AND USE THE STRUCTURE FOR SOME OTHER NEEDED CAPABILITY

The fourth course of action would be to decommission the remaining three Reserve F/A-18 squadrons and use this structure for some other more useful or needed capability. With the prospect of a declining defense budget in which equipment is being cut, it is hard to argue for a Reserve asset that has yet to be used since its inception into the Reserve system in 1991.[57] Though not recommended, this option in theory could free up some needed structure for some other low density, high demand type capability that could prove more helpful in the current GWOT.

One such example of this type of capability would be to use this gained structure for additional Reserve Civil Affairs Groups (CAG's). They are currently in high demand for use in the GWOT.[58] Another example would be to transition the squadrons into training and security battalions. There certainly is a need for this type of capability in the war on terror both in Iraq and Afghanistan, and there are simply not enough of these Marines to go around.

---

[57] Christopher P. Cavas, "Equipment Cuts Loom," *Marine Corps Times*, 17 January 05, 18.

[58] Civil Affairs Groups (CAG's) provide a wide variety of capabilities such as construction and public works projects, and civil and legal affairs to name a few. These units currently only reside in the Marine Corps Reserve. For more information see Christian Lowe, "5th CAG created for duty in Iraq," *Marine Corps Times*, 27 December 04, 15.

To make such a transition to a new capability would require having a two-sided approach, each requiring additional research and planning to make them efficient and effective. The first half of the plan would entail the disbanding of the remaining squadrons, which implies prior approval from both the SecDef and Congress, both of which may be difficult. There are procedures in place to take such action, but the big question going into such a plan would be what to do with the airplanes. The most likely scenario would have those F/A-18's transferred to the Active duty to supplement their inventory. Likewise, the Reserve pilots and mechanics could be offered an Active duty squadron affiliation, in which they would be able to still contribute to the total force, just through a different framework.[59] If this was determined not to be a viable option then they could simply try to find other billets in the Reserve system or transfer to the individual ready Reserve.

The other half of this plan, to transition the Reserve F/A-18's to an altogether different capability, would entail the restructuring portion. This portion of the plan would not be easy. There would need to be a separate staff from Manpower and Reserve Affairs assigned to access how best to go about doing this. A few of the issues would include: which type of capability is required, where would the manpower come from, and what site would be used to house this capability. Also, all the associated personnel, training, and fiscal responsibilities that come with each would have to be worked out. Like each of the other COA's, there are pros and cons with each option and this one is no different.

---

[59] The idea of affiliating the Reserve pilots and maintenance Marines into the Active duty squadrons is beyond the scope of this paper. Suffice to say this is done in the Air Force, and to some extent in the Navy both with varying degrees of success. More study and planning would be required to implement this option.

On the positives side, one can argue that by decommissioning the remaining Reserve F/A-18 squadrons, there would be a significant fiscal cost savings. This is only true to an extent. Most of the money associated with a Reserve squadron is known as "blue dollars" which is money that is appropriated for all the aviation associated items such as fuel, parts and aviation equipment. Though the average annual blue dollar budget for the typical Reserve hornet squadron is around ten million dollars, this cost savings would go back to the Navy.[60] The annual amount of money that the Marine Corps would realize in savings would only equate to around $400,000 dollars.[61] The bigger gain would not be realized fiscally, but rather in a potential higher demand warfighting capability.

When one looks at the negatives associated with this course of action, one realizes that there are two major detractors if this option were to be accepted. The first is that although $400,000 dollars sounds like a lot of money, in the grand scheme of defense spending, this amount is really very small. In fact, when one considers the capability that the Reserve F/A-18 squadrons provide, this is money well spent.

The second negative detractor that decommissioning the Reserve F/A-18 units would have would be manifested over time in the unintended consequences of this decision. The consequences of such a decision could have second and third order effects that could possibly result in the loss of Marine Tactical Aviation throughout the Marine Corps. If that were to happen, the Marine Corps would look more and more like the Army, which could prove to be the first step in another age-old battle for the Marine Corps existence. Though a viable option, this would not be the recommend course of action for the Marine leadership to take.

---

[60] Col Blalock interview.
[61] MGen Ghormley interview.

> *"Without Air there is no MAGTF."*
>
> > *--General Charles Krulak*
> > *31st Commandant of the Marine Corps*
>
> *"It's the first step [not using the Reserve TacAir Squadrons] along the way to becoming Amphibious Rangers."*
>
> > *--MGen Ghormley*
> > *Director Manpower Plans and Policy Division, Dec 2004*

COA #5: **MAINTAIN THE STATUS QUO AND FACE THEIR POSSIBLE LOSS**

The final option is to do nothing and maintain the status quo, thus leaving the Marine Reserve F/A-18 squadrons on the shelf. This decision, which pragmatically stems from indecision, could leave the Marine Corps with some unintended consequences. This course of action is not the recommended path to follow for the following three reasons. First, the nation is in the middle of a protracted war against a global transnational threat. The resulting effect of combating this threat is that the Active duty Marine Corps is operating at nearly a 1-to-1 contingency deployment cycle, which left unadjusted will create a potentially huge force sustainment problem. The irregular warfare terrorist attacks of 9-11 changed the character of war in which the military is finding itself fully immersed. The problem is, unlike traditional warfare, there is no indication of how long it will last; some guess 5, 10, 15 years at the very least. In this context of reality, there is no logical reason why the Marine Corps should not use all of the forces available. An unconventional, asymmetric, protracted war will require the use of all available forces to help carry the load if America intends to win the peace.

Next, if the Reserve F/A-18s are not used, then a personnel problem in the Reserve TacAir side will also emerge. These Marines voluntarily joined the Reserves for a reason: to help defend America and its values in times of war. The GWOT is such a time, and if they are not going to be used, then they will look to find a unit someplace else to accomplish what they have set out to do.[62] Or, they will simply quit. Either way, the impact will be felt, and it is just a matter of time before it starts to happen.

Finally, and most importantly, inaction will have the unintended consequences of the F/A-18 squadrons losing their relevancy.[63] Leaving this capability on the shelf during a time of war, especially when the Active force is being subjected to ever increasing operations tempo, will likely led to the first step in losing these forces.[64] Therefore, the Marine Corps as and institution needs to make a corporate decision of what the future Corps should look like 15-20 years from now.

Should the Marine Corps continue to have a fixed wing TacAir capability inherent in the aviation portion of the MAGTF? Or is only having rotary wing support going to be sufficient to support the ground combat element? If the answer is that the Marine Corps believes that rotary wing support is all that is necessary, then this COA could be the first step in making that happen. For not mobilizing the Reserve hornets can lead to their loss. If TacAir assets are not required in the Reserves, then the skeptics can argue; why are TacAir assets required in the Active force? The result of this could be that the MAGTF may be left with only rotary wing aircraft to support the ground combat element, and the Marine Corps MAGTF capability would be significantly reduced. One may just as well change the Marine's name to "Amphibious Rangers," for the only capabilities the Marine Corps would have to differentiate themselves from the Army would be their

---

[62] Col Blalock interview.
[63] Col Blalock interview.
[64] MGen Ghormley interview.

expeditionary and amphibious nature.[65] If the loss of Marine TacAir was allowed to

happen, a third argument could be made that this TacAir loss could lead to the

abolishment of the MAGTF and therefore the Marine Corps all together.

---

[65] MGen Ghormley interview.

CHAPTER #4

> *"We all [the U.S. Military] are worried about the stress on the force."*
>
> *--MGen Bergman*
> *Director of Manpower and Reserve Affairs*
>
> *"The steady state of the next three to five years will find Reserve components supporting operations Noble Eagle, Enduring Freedom, and Iraqi Freedom, and other operations with a total of about 100,000 to 150,000 personnel. ...Mobilizations of up to one year or more will be the norm for Reserve component members during the next three to five years."*
>
> *--Pentagon Office of Reserve Affairs Report*

SUMMARY

This analysis has provided the answers to the questions of the Marine Reserve F/A-18 squadron's relevancy, and why, to date, those units have not been used in the Global War on Terror. Also discussed were the issues that influenced the Marine Corps decision makers thought processes when the initial OIF Reserve force mobilization decisions were being made. Upon this background, five possible courses of action were offered, which if implemented by the decision makers, the Marine Corps can significantly improve the use of the Marine Reserve F/A-18 unit's capability.

The first and recommended course of action is the most likely, that is to mobilize the Reserve F/A-18 squadrons for use in the Global War on Terror. This option provides present day Active duty optempo relief while ensuring the relevancy of Marine Reserve TacAir for the foreseeable future. The second, third, and fourth courses of action were options that required some transformational changes in the way the Marine Corps leadership viewed problems. Each of these were conceptual options and would require some addition planning and research, but if implemented could have a significant impact on the total force construct while increasing the Marine Corps total warfighting capability for the future. The final course of action is the most dangerous; it is the option of indecision. If the Marine leadership is willing to maintain the status quo as suggested by COA #5, then they must also be prepared to endure the possible unintended consequences of this decision, namely the possible loss of the Reserve F/A-18 squadrons.

There are three distinct take-a-ways that the reader should obtain from this Reserve F/A-18 squadron relevancy analysis. First, the Marine Reserve F/A-18 units are relevant to the Marine Corps and its total force construct. They provide the same, and arguably an enhanced, combat capability that their Active duty counter-parts provide. The problem lies in the fact that these forces remain under utilized. It's hard for the Reserve F/A-18 squadrons to be able to assist the Combatant Commander, and, therefore, the nation, in accomplishing their GWOT mission objectives when they are not activated.

Secondly, to date, the reasons why the Reserve F/A-18 squadrons have not been used to support the GWOT are complicated. Suffice it to say, they were not used for a variety of reasons which can be summed up as a combination of politics, policy, and the service culture, all having the by-product equating to an over arching fear to mobilize these resources. The resulting effect was that a shortsighted decision was made on the basis of these policies and service culture, as well as a valid assumption, which turned out to be wildly incorrect.

The political, statutory, policy, and the cultural barriers currently in place to protect the nation's "citizen soldiers" need to be addressed. It seems the mindset currently in vogue, when decisions regarding the Reserve forces are made, is a hold over from the post Vietnam Cold War era. The attacks of 9-11 changed the character of today's warfare from that of fighting the big conventional war with the Soviets, to an unconventional war against transnational terrorist threats. So, too, must the mindset of the people, government, and the military change. This is especially the case when discussing the total force issues involved with mobilization of the nation's Reserve forces. To quote Abraham Lincoln, whose words apply today as they did when he addressed Congress in December 1862, "As our case is new, so we must think anew, and act anew."[66] The Marine Corps leadership must also think anew when making the decisions regarding the mobilization of the Reserve forces for use in the extended Global War on Terror. If the constraints and restraints imposed by the policies, statues, and cultural paradeigms are not fixed, the result could be a broken military force both Active and Reserve. Additionally, Reserve component education should be instituted at all levels of formal schooling to help break down some of the cultural walls between the Active and Reserve Marines. Thus, the time is now to look long range and mobilize the Reserve F/A-18 squadrons for use in the GWOT.

Finally, and most importantly, the Marine Corps as an institution needs to make a corporate decision of what the future Corps should look like 15-20 years from now. Should the Marine Corps continue to have a fixed wing TacAir capability inherent in the aviation portion of the MAGTF? Or is having only rotary wing support going to be sufficient enough for the ground combat element? By making this decision, the leadership will be better armed to make the shaping decisions required today, to properly affect the future without having unintended consequences. Therefore, the Marine Corps will continue to be the "Nations Force in Readiness" while enduring the test of time.

---

[66] Abraham Lincon (1809-1865), U.S. president annual message to Congress, 1 December 1862, *Collected Works of Abraham Lincoln*, vol. 5, (Rutgers University Press 1953,1990), 537.

CONCLUSION

It is clear from this analysis that the Marine Reserve F/A-18 squadrons are relevant and Headquarters Marine Corps should mobilize the 4th MAW Squadrons for use in Operation Iraqi freedom and support of the Global War on Terror. In doing so, the Marine leadership will validate the Reserve TacAir total force construct, while ensuring the Tactical Aviation portion of the "A" in the Marine Air Ground Task Force remains a pillar of relevancy. But, the window of opportunity to make this decision is getting smaller and smaller, and time is not a virtue in this case. The more time that passes without Reserve TacAir being mobilized, the stronger the argument becomes to transform this structure into some other capability, or do away with it all together.

The decision makers must act, and act soon, or face the reality that the Marine Corps as an institution could lose the Reserve TacAir structure. This potential loss could have unwanted second and third order outcomes, ultimately, providing the Marine Aviation skeptics the ammunition they want and need to do away with Marine Corps TacAir entirely. If TacAir assets are not required in the Reserves, then the skeptics can argue, why is TacAir required in the Active force? It is commonplace to be in-battled in a continuous political struggle for monies in the world of military jointness. The Marine Corps may find itself both politically and institutionally up against the budgetary wall. The result of this could leave the MAGTF with only rotary wing aircraft to support the ground combat element, and the Marine Corps MAGTF capability would be significantly reduced.

This could signal the start of the end of the Marine Corps as it exists today, and one may just as well change the Marines name to "Amphibious Rangers," for the only capabilities the Marine Corps would have to differentiate themselves from the Army would be their expeditionary and amphibious nature.[67] If the loss of Marine TacAir was allowed to happen, a third order consequence of this loss could in time lead to the total abolishment of the MAGTF, and therefore the Marine Corps service as a whole. So, the time is at hand to make the honorable decision, mobilize the Reserve F/A-18's, or face the realities of inaction.

Thucydides stated that decisions concerning war in democracies are made based on "fear, honor, and interest."[68] It can be argued that, like the era of the Peloponnesian War in 432 B.C., the same set of criteria hold true today. The Marine Corps leadership, out of fear and their own political interests, made what they thought to be the honorable decision when they decided not to mobilize the Reserve F/A-18 squadrons for use in Operation Iraqi Freedom. Although shortsighted, it was a reasonable decision when one considers the time and circumstance. Now, with the U.S. military facing the extensive war on terror, a new set of circumstances has evolved. In light of this new context, the honorable decision for the Marine leadership is to mobilize 4th MAW F/A-18 squadrons for use in the GWOT.

In doing so, the total force would benefit by having a reduced operational tempo for the Active duty Marine F/A-18 squadrons. Also, the Marine Corps as an institution

---

[67] MGen Ghormley interview.
[68] Richard B. Strassler, Ed., *The Landmark Thucydides: A Comprehensive Guide to the Pelopennesian War,* (New York: Free Press, 1996), 43.

will secure the relevance of Marine Tactical Aviation. This decision would solidify the Marine Corps' most basic warfighting concept. By keeping TacAir in the Aviation element of the MAGTF, the entire combat package the Marine Corps provides to the Combatant Commander, will continue to thrive for the foreseeable future. If no action is taken, the first step towards losing TacAir may be effectively completed and this stepping-stone could lead toward making the Marine Corps an "Amphibious Ranger Force." The time is at hand to make the honorable decision. Mobilize the Reserve F/A-18 squadrons, or face the realities of inaction. Let the debate begin.

Bibliography

Amos, James F., LtGen, USMC. Commanding General II Marine Expeditionary Force. Headquarters II MEF, Camp Lejeune, NC. Telephone interview by the author, 03 December 2004.

Balkcom, Chritopher and O'Rourke, Ronald. *Navy-Marine Corps Tactical Air Integration.* CRS *Report for Congress* RS21488. Washington, DC: Congressional Research Service, The Library of Congress, 10 April 2003.

Bergman, John W., MGen, USMCR. Director, Reserve Affairs, Manpower and Reserve Affairs, Headquarters Marine Corps, Quantico, VA. Interview by the author, 6 December 2004.

Blalock, William, P., Col, USMCR. Deputy Commander MAG-41, JRB Fort-Worth, TX. Interview by the author, 10 January 2005.

Bowman, Tom. "Army Reserve Fast Becoming Broken Force." *Baltimore Sun,* 05 January 2005, A1+.

Brady, Robert M., Col, USMC. Director, Aviation Plans and Policy, Headquarters Marine Corps, Washington, DC. Interview by the author, 01 December 2004.

Brinkley, Mark. "The Way Ahead; After Iraq, top Marine sets a course for resetting the force and beyond." *Marine Corps Times*, 13 October 2003, 1+.

Cavas, Christopher P. "Equipment Cuts Loom." *Marine Corps Times*, 17 January 2005, 18+.

Cebrowski, Arthur. "Transformation and The Changing Character of War." *ROA National Security Report*, July/August 2004, 1-3.

Crawley, Vince. "GAO REPORT SAYS: Reserve well running dry." *Marine Corps Times,* 04 October 2004, 24+.

"Reservists face a busy outlook." *Marine Corps Times,* 04 October 2004, 8.

Coombs, Danial P., Maj, USMC. Command and Staff College Masters Thesis Paper. *Reserve Integration: A Corps Competency.* Quantico, VA: Gray Research Center, 2003.

Department of Defense Directive 5100.1. *Functions of the Department of Defense and Its Major Components.* Washington, DC: U.S. Government Printing Office, 01 August 2003.

Department of Defense. *Role of Reserve TacAir.* Publication L. No 108-87, section 8141. Washington, DC: U.S. Government Printing Office, 2003.

Education Center, Marine Corps Development and Education Command. *Categories of Reserve.* Quantico, VA: U.S. Marine Corps, 1980.

Education Center, Marine Corps Development and Education Command. *Marine Reserve Mobilization.* Quantico, VA: U.S. Marine Corps, 1980.

Education Center, Marine Corps Development and Education Command. *The Fourth Division Wing Team.* Quantico, VA: U.S. Marine Corps, 1980.

Education Center, Marine Corps Development and Education Command. *The Marine Corps Reserve, A Short History.* Quantico, VA: U.S. Marine Corps, 1980.

Education Center, Marine Corps Development and Education Command. *The Total Force Marine Corps.* Quantico, VA: U.S. Marine Corps, 1979.

Ford, W.G. "Cowboys Tame the Far East: VMFA-112," *Leatherneck*, Volume 87, Issue 10, October 2004, 26-28.

Garand, George, and Strobridge, Truman. *Western Pacific Operations; History of U.S. Marine Corps Operations in World War II. Vol. IV.* Washington, DC: U.S. Government Printing Office, 1970.

Garick, Sean B. "Enough Marine Air on Carriers Already." *Proceedings of the United States Naval Institute*, August 2002, 3+.

Gertz, Bill and Scarborough, Rowan. "Cinc Lives." *Washington Times*, 18 September 2003, A1+.

Ghormley, Timothy F., MGen, USMC. Director, Manpower Plans and Policy Division, Manpower and Reserve Affairs, Headquarters Marine Corps, Quantico, VA. Interview by the author, 06 December 2004.

Hawkins, Mantford C., Col, USMC. Commanding Officer MAG-41, JRB Fort-Worth, TX. Telephone interview by the author, 08 December 2004.

Headquarters Marine Corps, Programs and Resources Department. *Marine Corps Concepts and Programs 2004.* N.p., 2004, 97-99.

Hitchcock, David M., LtCol, USMC. TacAir Plans, Department of Aviation, Headquarters Marine Corps, Washington, DC. Interview by the author, 22 September 2004.

Hough, Mike, LtGen, USMC. "The Future of Marine Corps Aviation." *Naval Aviation News,* May-June 2003, Volume 85, Issue 4, 8.

Jane's: All the Worlds Aircraft 2001-2002. Eds. Paul Jackson and others. Surrey, UK: Sentinel House, 2002.

Jenkins, Dennis R. *The F/A-18 Hornet, A Navy Success Story.* Washington, DC: McGraw-Hill, 2000.

Joint Publication, JP 0-2. *Unified Action Armed Forces (UNAAF).* N.p., 10 July 2001.

Joint Publication, JP 1-02. *Department of Defense Dictionary of Military and Associated Terms.* N.p., 5 June 2003.

Joint Publication, JP 4-05.1. *Reserve Component Decision Making Process.* N.p., 11 November 1998.

Joint Publication, JP 5-00.1. *Joint Doctrine for Campaign Planning.* N.p., 25 January 2002.

Lincon, Abraham, (1809-1865). U.S. president annual message to Congress, 1 December 1862. *Collected Works of Abraham Lincoln*, vol. 5. Rutgers University Press 1953,1990. 537.

Lowe, Christian. "5th CAG created for duty in Iraq." *Marine Corps Times*, 27 December 2004, 15.

    "Reserve official: Revamp the Force." *Marine Corps Times*, 08 September 2003, 44.

Marine Corps Doctrine Publication. MCDP 1-0. *Marine Corps Operations.* N.p., September 2001.

Mahnken, Thomas G. and Fitzsimonds, James R. "Tread-Heads or Technophiles? Army Officer Attitudes Toward Transformation." *Parameters,* Summer 2004, 57-72.

Marine Corps Historical Reference Pamphlet. *Mobilization of the Marine Corps Reserve in the Korean Conflict, 1950-1951.* Washington, DC: Historical Branch, G-3 Division Headquarters, U. S. Marine Corps, 1967.

Marine Corps Reserve Guidebook, Section V, Paragraph 1. *Manpower and Reserve Affairs Home Page*, https://Inweb1.manpower.usmc.mil. Web URL address http://mcrsc.mfr.usmc.mil/Guidebook/Guidbook.asp., accessed 27 December 2004.

McCarthy, Dennis M., LtGen, USMCR. Commanding General Marine Forces Reserve. Headquarters Marine Forces Reserve, New Orleans, LA. Interview by the author, 27 February 2005.

McCarthy, Dennis M., LtGen, USMCR. "Marine Forces Reserve." *Marine Corps Gazette,* March 2004, 12.

Mersky, Peter. *U.S. Marine Corps Aviation, 1912 to the Present.* Baltimore, MD: The Nautical & Aviation Publishing Company of America, 1983.

Morey, David B., Col, USMC. Staff SJA Mobilization Command. Headquarters Marine Corps, Kansas City, MO. Telephone interview by the author, 02 March 2005.

Parker, George. "Letter From Baghdad, War after War." *The New Yorker Magazine.* 24 November 2003, 52-58.

Phillips, Gary et. al. "Marine Aviation Requirements Study: Summary Report." *CNR Research Memorandum CRM D0003922.A2/Final,* August 2001.

Post, Martin, Bgen, USMC. Assistant Deputy Commandant Aviation. Department of Aviation, Headquarters Marine Corps, Washington, DC. Interview by the author, 10 September 2004.

"Reserve Mobilizations." *Marine Corps Times,* 17 November 2003, 38.

Reserve Officers of Public Affairs Unit 4-1. *The Marine Corps Reserve, A History.* Washington, DC: Division of Reserve, Headquarters, U.S. Marine Corps, 1966.

Roach, Donald, Maj, USMC. Inspector and Instructor staff, VMFA-321, MAG-49, 4th Marine Aircraft Wing, Andrews AFB, MD. Interview by the author, 08 September 2004.

Shermen, Jason. "Rolling QDR Could Shape 05 Budget." *Defense News,* 6 December 2004, 1+.

"U.S. Seeks to add Flex to Force." *Defense News,* 6 September 2004, 8+.

Sherrod, Robert. *History of Marine Corps Aviation in WWII.* Washington, DC: Combat Force Press, 1952.

Strassler, Richard B., Ed. *The Landmark Thucydides: A Comprehensive Guide to the Peloponnesian War.* New York: Free Press, 1996.

Training and Education Command, United States Marine Corps. *F/A-18 Training and Readiness Manual (T&R), MCO 3500.46.* 10 September 2004. *Marine Corps Training and Education Command Home Page,* www.tecom.usmc.mil. Web URL address www.usmc.mil/directivnsf/mco?., accessed 5 January 2005.

Tustin, Adam. *Reserve Activations Reach Highest Since Korea,* July 2004. *Marine Forces Reserve Home Page,* www.mfr.usmc.mil. Web URL address "http://www.marforres.usmc.mil/Archive/2004.07/activations.html.," accessed 13 August 2004.

United States Code. Title 10, section 101, 262, 12302. *Armed Forces of the United States.* Washington, DC: GPO, 2 January 2001.

Under Secretary of Defense, Personnel and Readiness (P&R). Memorandum for the Assistant Secretary of the Army (M&RA), Navy (M&RA), and Air Force (SAF/MR). Subject: "Mobilization / Demobilization Personnel and Pay Policy for Reserve Component Members Ordered to Active Duty in Response to the World Trade Center and Pentagon Attacks." 20 September 2001.

United States Government Accountability Office Report to Congressional Committees. *Force Structure: Department of the Navy's Tactical Aviation Integration Plan is Reasonable, but Some Factors Could Affect Implementation.* GAO 04-900. Washington, DC: Government Accountability Office, August 2004.

United States Government Accountability Office Report to Congressional Committees. Military Personnel: *A Strategic Approach is Needed to Address Long-Term Guard and Reserve Force Availability.* GAO-05-285T. Washington, DC: Government Accountability Office, February 2005.

United States Government Accountability Office Report to Congressional Committees. *Military Personnel: DOD Needs to Address Long-term Reserve Force Availability and Related Mobilization and Demobilization Issues.* GAO 04-1031. Washington, DC: Government Accountability Office, September 2004.

United States Marine Corps, Marine Forces Reserve. *History of VMFA-321. Marine Forces Reserve Home Page,* www.mfr.usmc.mil. Web URL address http://www.mfr.usmc.mil/4thmaw/mag49/vmfa321/, accessed 13 September 2004.

U. S. President. Executive Order 13223. "President Orders Ready Reserve of Armed Forces to Active Duty." 14 September 2001.

Worley, Robert. *Marine Corps.* N.p., undated manuscript draft. Warfighting From the Sea, MAGTF Organization Syllabus, AY 2004-2005.

www.ingramcontent.com/pod-product-compliance
Lightning Source LLC
Chambersburg PA
CBHW080608290526
45790CB00007B/2686